This Journal Belongs To

Made in United States
Orlando, FL
02 May 2022

17407267R00063